Oprah's
THE LIFE YOU WANT

LOVE AND HAPPINESS
JOURNAL

TALKING TO THOUSANDS of people over the years has shown me that there is one desire we all share: Each of us at our core longs to be loved—to have intimate connections that leave us feeling more alive, more human. As Maya Angelou—who taught me so much— said in the quote you'll find on page 6, love is the condition in the human spirit that is the basis for so much in our lives: strength, courage, kindness. We're all striving for authenticity in our relationships, for true spirit-to-spirit connections. While achieving that requires serious emotional work, at this moment in time, doesn't it feel more important than ever to cultivate love, to seek it out in all its forms?

I believe that when you make loving others the story of your life, you begin to reach toward your highest potential. And, as you lend your light to one person, they shine it on another and another and another. Of course, before we can love others, we must first find a way to love ourselves—no small thing. But when I see moments of conflict or hatred—small or community wide—I think we have an opportunity to reimagine our traditional idea of love: to broaden beyond the feelings we hold for our partners, children, and friends and expand our capacity for love to those who share our journey on this planet.

With all this in mind, we at Oprah Daily created this journal to help you find more fulfillment in your relationships, bring more love into your life, and increase connection in our larger world. Too often, I've seen people pining for love—from an unreachable parent, from a romantic partner—or seeking simply to be rescued from their lives, despite the fact that all around them are neighbors, friends, children, trusted colleagues, and even strangers with whom they have moments of genuine connection.

So our first chapter is a **Love Inventory,** an opportunity to acknowledge the love that's being shared with you right now. After that, you'll move through 11 more chapters, each focused on exploring values that I believe are foundational to establishing trusted relationships across our lives—from seeing others clearly and developing appreciation to recognizing chosen family and extending love into our imperfect world. Supporting each theme are exercises designed to help you identify opportunities for true kinship (and for highlighting blind spots that may be holding you back). Each chapter builds on the prior exercises, so that you can track your progress as you incorporate these techniques into your daily life. Finally, I've been fortunate to learn about love from many wise people in our world— those who came on *The Oprah Winfrey Show*, joined us at live events across the country, shared wisdom in the pages of *O, The Oprah Magazine*, and some who sat down among the oaks and talked with me. You will find some of their most inspiring quotes throughout these pages.

I hope that this journal helps you realize that your greatest power is your ability to love—to show it, to receive it, and to validate others. Let's begin...

TABLE OF
Contents

INTRODUCTION 7

CHAPTER ONE: A Love Inventory 11

CHAPTER TWO: Choosing to Love Oneself 27

CHAPTER THREE: Seeing Others Clearly 49

CHAPTER FOUR: Giving Your Attention 69

CHAPTER FIVE: Choosing Appreciation 85

CHAPTER SIX: Setting Boundaries 99

CHAPTER SEVEN: Finding Courage 115

CHAPTER EIGHT: Improving Communication 129

CHAPTER NINE: Recognizing Chosen Family 145

CHAPTER TEN: Embracing Romantic Love 159

CHAPTER ELEVEN: Redefining Parenthood 171

CHAPTER TWELVE: Practicing Lovingkindness 183

LOVE INVENTORY: Reflection 194

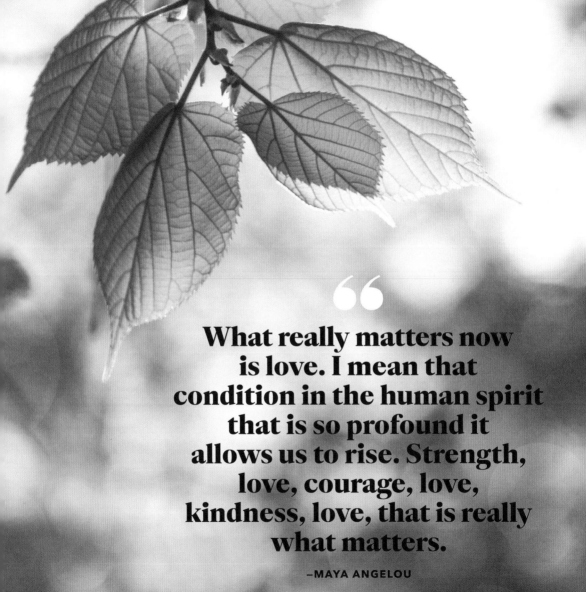

> **What really matters now is love. I mean that condition in the human spirit that is so profound it allows us to rise. Strength, love, courage, love, kindness, love, that is really what matters.**
>
> —MAYA ANGELOU

INTRODUCTION
How to Use this Journal

Don Miguel Ruiz once wrote that "To become masters of love, we have to practice love." That's what this journal offers: a chance to think about how you might better practice love so you can share yourself in the best ways possible with the people you care most about.

It includes 12 themed lessons, with several exercises to complete over the course of about a month. Many of these exercises build upon each other—meaning the work you do early will be revisited— so take your time in answering the prompts. That might mean finding a quiet moment before your day gets crazy to read one of the opening essays, or spending time with an exercise before committing words to paper. Feel free to move at your own pace— you might want to reflect on one exercise for a few days before answering, spend more time on some chapters than others, take a break when needed...after all, love isn't in a rush.

Here are the three types of prompts you'll see and how they will lead you to deeper connections:

FILL IN THE BLANKS

These questions offer an opportunity for thoughtful examination of where you are now regarding the relationships in your life—and where you hope to be.

VISUAL EXERCISES

These exercises allow you to see your life in a new perspective and make visible certain patterns you may not have noticed before.

AHA MOMENTS

At the end of each chapter, you'll have a chance to reflect on the themed lesson. Whatever works for you is right, so open up your heart on these pages any way you like.

For more inspiration and guidance on how to bring more love, in all its forms, into your life, visit OprahDaily.com.

VISION BOARD
Your Heart Space

Before we create our **Love Inventory,**
let's take a quick moment to make visible the
invisible connections you currently have.

STEP 1:

Begin by dividing the left circle into sections representing
the amount of love and attention you would ideally like
to commit to the people and practices in your life (romantic
partner, family, friends, work, spiritual practice, etc.).

STEP 2:

Now divide the second circle to indicate where your love and attention are *actually* invested today. Keep this exercise in mind as you do the work in the upcoming chapters, reflecting especially on how those exercises might help you move toward a life that embodies the left heart divisions.

"

Wherever you've
been touched by love,
a heartprint lingers.

—OPRAH

CHAPTER ONE

A Love Inventory

When most of us think about expanding the love in our lives, we focus on Big Romantic Love or Finding Our Soulmate. Remember, though: The chance to love and be loved exists at almost any moment in your life. Most of us can't see it, because we have our own preconceived ideas about what love is and how it should appear in our lives. Yet love can be found with friends, with family, in tiny moments with strangers, and within relationships that last a lifetime. So let's start with an inventory of the times when you were cared for, when someone showed you that you mattered—the reminders of the love that's available to you right now.

Turn the page for the first set of exercises. Feel free to move at your own pace through each one. Then take a moment to consider what you've learned before moving on to the next chapter.

IDENTIFY THE LOVE YOU HAVE

The first step is to put a check mark next to all the instances where you've been shown love recently. This exercise is a starting point— one that you'll refer back to in subsequent chapters—so I encourage you to take your time in capturing the encounters of care shown to you. These could be with friends, family, your partner, a trusted colleague, or a stranger.

For instance, when someone...

- Gave you a sense of safety
- Really listened to you
- Expanded your world with new people, ideas, or activities
- Made you laugh
- Came to your defense
- Showed that they knew you better than anyone
- Was there for you
- Handled things you're not good at
- Encouraged you to pursue your interest
- Was vulnerable with you
- Did what they said they would do
- Accepted your less-kind moments
- Showed kindness toward you
- Took your needs or wants into consideration
- Expressed what they honestly felt

ACKNOWLEDGE MOMENTS BIG AND SMALL

Take a moment to delve deeper into ten of the aspects you checked. This will push you to acknowledge moments, especially small or unexpected ones, that you may have overlooked.

Type of love:

_____

_____

_____

_____

_____

_____

Who gave it:

_____

A favorite instance of this is when they:

_____

_____

_____

_____

_____

_____

Type of love:

_____

_____

_____

_____

_____

_____

Who gave it:

_____

A favorite instance of this is when they:

_____

_____

_____

_____

_____

_____

CONTINUED →

Type of love:

_____

_____

_____

Who gave it:

_____

A favorite instance of this is when they:

_____

_____

_____

_____

Type of love:

_____

_____

_____

Who gave it:

_____

A favorite instance of this is when they:

_____

_____

_____

_____

Type of love:

_____

_____

_____

Who gave it:

_____

A favorite instance of this is when they:

_____

_____

_____

_____

Type of love:

_____

_____

_____

Who gave it:

_____

A favorite instance of this is when they:

_____

_____

_____

_____

Type of love:

_____

_____

_____

Who gave it:

_____

A favorite instance of this is when they:

_____

_____

_____

_____

Type of love:

_____

_____

_____

Who gave it:

_____

A favorite instance of this is when they:

_____

_____

_____

_____

Type of love:

_____

_____

_____

Who gave it:

_____

A favorite instance of this is when they:

_____

_____

_____

_____

Type of love:

_____

_____

_____

Who gave it:

_____

A favorite instance of this is when they:

_____

_____

_____

_____

REVEAL WHAT'S MISSING

Now that you have a sense of the love that's shown to you, look through your answers to the first two exercises, and ask yourself if there are types of love you're missing from others. What types of love do you hope to cultivate as you work through this journal?

Type of love that's missing:

_____

_____

_____

_____

_____

_____

Why you want to have it:

_____

_____

_____

_____

_____

_____

_____

_____

Type of love that's missing:

_____

_____

_____

_____

_____

_____

Why you want to have it:

_____

_____

_____

_____

_____

_____

_____

_____

Type of love that's missing:

_____

_____

_____

Why you want to have it:

_____

_____

_____

_____

_____

_____

Type of love that's missing:

_____

_____

_____

Why you want to have it:

_____

_____

_____

_____

_____

_____

Type of love that's missing:

_____

_____

_____

Why you want to have it:

_____

_____

_____

_____

_____

_____

Type of love that's missing:

_____

_____

_____

Why you want to have it:

_____

_____

_____

_____

_____

_____

RECALL WHAT YOU SHARED

Now let's think about the moments in your life when you've shown love to others. Put a check next to ten of the expressions of love and respect listed below that you think are the most meaningful to the people you love. Then put a check next to the ten that are most natural for you.

MEANINGFUL		NATURAL
○	Listen without interrupting	○
○	Allow them their opinions	○
○	Courteously disagree	○
○	Tell them the truth	○
○	Apologize when you're wrong	○
○	Let them know if they've offended you	○
○	Celebrate their wins	○
○	Keep your word	○
○	Offer help when it seems appropriate	○
○	Give them room to learn from mistakes	○
○	Keep them in the loop/informed	○
○	Be patient/hold your temper	○
○	Validate their point of view and contributions	○
○	Keep their secrets	○
○	Show interest in their welfare and their lives	○
○	Promptly return their things in good order or replace them	○
○	Encourage and mentor	○
○	Try to understand and accept different perspectives	○
○	Bring an open mind to interactions	○
○	Be inclusive	○
○	Give praise freely	○

CHART YOUR ANSWERS

Look at your answers on prior pages. In which areas of your life do you feel you are receiving and sharing enough love? Place a check mark in each row to indicate what feels accurate now. We'll come back to this exercise at the end of the journal. The goal is to move checks to the left— from enough to abundance, from absent to enough.

	ABUNDANCE OF LOVE	ENOUGH LOVE	NEED MORE LOVE
Friends			
Family			
Children			
Acquaintances			
Romantic Partner			
Spiritual Love			

THIS IS YOUR STARTING POINT

Over the next chapters, you'll begin to build on this foundation to discover who and what make you feel most loved as well as to learn who and what could use more of your love.

AHA MOMENTS...

Now that you've completed this chapter, think of these pages as an opportunity to go a little deeper. **What have you realized about...**

How much love you have now?

_____

_____

_____

_____

_____

_____

_____

_____

_____

_____

_____

How much love you share?

_____

_____

_____

_____

_____

_____

_____

_____

_____

_____

_____

_____

The areas where you feel that you lack love?

_____

_____

_____

_____

_____

_____

_____

_____

_____

_____

_____

_____

_____

_____

_____

_____

_____

_____

_____

_____

_____

_____

66

The moment we choose to love we begin to move toward freedom...

–BELL HOOKS

Notes

Notes

If you feel incomplete, you alone must fill all your empty, shattered places with love.

—OPRAH

CHAPTER TWO
Choosing to Love Oneself

To love who you are means knowing who you are. It's the foundation for wholeness. When you connect with the source inside yourself, your life becomes clearer. You know what matters to you...what makes your heart sing... what you can and want to offer to others and the world. But I've seen so many people who are looking for someone else to make their lives whole. Sometimes they mean having a child, but mostly they're seeking a romantic partner. It's the "you complete me" illusion—you know the one—and it's just that: an illusion, and a dangerous one. Because when you think about it, you alone make a whole person. If you feel incomplete, you, alone, must fill yourself with love. Instead of focusing on what you aren't getting from others, take the opportunity to ask yourself where you need to love yourself more—and decide how you might work on welcoming your own love.

LOOK INSIDE

Knowing and loving yourself starts by exploring the inner you—your inward swirl of emotions, energies, and abilities. Connecting to that essential source of love is a key step in feeling that you are a being worthy of love.

STEP 1:

In the space around the dot at right, write words or phrases—or if you can't find the words, draw a sketch—that describe the best version of your inner self. Skip external definitions, like "boss," "activist," or "expert knitter." Focus on your yearnings, your joys, your emotions, the feelings you carry in your heart, the hopes that drive you. This is the opposite of writing a checklist of things you do, like "donates to charity." Instead, replace these activities with internal values—maybe "a giving person."

It might help to lie down, close your eyes, take three deep breaths, and let your mind take flight.

STEP 2:

Are there themes or patterns that you were previously unaware of?

_____

_____

_____

_____

_____

_____

_____

_____

_____

_____

BUILD A FOUNDATION

The more you trust yourself, the better you take care of yourself. The better you take care of yourself, the more trustworthy you'll be with others. Complete the following sentence:

I trust myself...

- Most of the time
- Kind of/sometimes
- Not very often

What happens when self-trust isn't there? Check any that sound true for you.

- I go back and forth before making decisions
- I change direction in the middle of something
- I let other people take control
- I do things that prevent me from getting what I want
- I second-guess my decisions in a big way
- I make a big deal out of small things
- I make other people feel bad
- I do this: _____

If your compassion does not include yourself, it is incomplete.

–JACK KORNFIELD

Think of a situation when lack of self-trust got in your way. If you could rewind the clock, what is one small thing you would do differently?

_____

_____

_____

_____

_____

_____

_____

How could you apply that small change in the future?

_____

_____

_____

_____

_____

_____

_____

How will that help you trust yourself more?

_____

_____

_____

_____

_____

_____

_____

CHOOSE SELF-RESPECT

The author Joan Didion said that "character—the willingness to accept responsibility for one's own life—is the source from which self-respect springs." Take a moment to think about the ways you show up for yourself.

Start by listing the ways you take responsibility for yourself. This could include things like speaking gently to yourself, organizing your closets, setting boundaries, paying your bills, or taking credit for doing something well.

Now list the actions or experiences in which you haven't accepted responsibility for your thoughts or actions—you didn't keep your word, you were late to meetings, you chose jealousy over joy for a friend's success.

What do the first category items have in common? Is it that you felt confident in those skills?

_____

_____

_____

_____

_____

_____

_____

_____

_____

_____

_____

_____

_____

_____

_____

_____

_____

_____

_____

_____

_____

_____

_____

_____

_____

What do the items where you let yourself down have in common? Is it that you were insecure or overwhelmed?

_____

_____

_____

_____

_____

_____

_____

_____

_____

_____

_____

_____

_____

_____

_____

_____

_____

_____

_____

_____

_____

_____

_____

_____

_____

What actions might you take that will make you feel loved when you find yourself in the more challenging circumstances? Maybe take a walk (even if your to-do list isn't finished) or give yourself a small, unexpected treat (a nicer-than-usual pen, a fancier coffee, a call to a friend). Take a photo of your answer with your phone or rewrite it on a piece of paper you can carry in your wallet so you can easily access it whenever you need it.

EXTEND COMPASSION

The capacity for true intimacy is based on self-acceptance. One path to self-acceptance is to extend compassion to oneself. How do you show up for yourself? Reflect on a past situation in which you really needed compassion.

What was the situation?

What did you think that made you feel better in that moment?

What did you think that did not make you feel better?

🖎 Circle the thought that had the most staying power.

CONTINUED →

In that same situation, what did you do that made you feel better?

What did you do that did *not* make you feel better?

✏️ **Circle the action you remember most.**

Again, recalling that same situation... Why did you feel badly?

○ I was measuring myself against someone else's success.

○ I was judging myself against what I've been told is the right way to respond.

○ I was comparing myself to what I've done in the past when I've been more in control.

○ Other: _____

_____

_____

_____

_____

Write down what you would say and do for a good friend who has disappointed herself.

_____

_____

_____

_____

_____

_____

_____

_____

_____

_____

_____

_____

Look back at your earlier answers. Is that what you said to or did for yourself?

_____

_____

_____

_____

_____

_____

_____

_____

_____

_____

_____

_____

_____

CONTINUED →

Based on what you've learned from looking back at your earlier answers, how will you handle future moments so that you can encourage self-acceptance and boost your self-compassion?

_____

_____

_____

_____

_____

_____

_____

_____

_____

_____

List five positive affirmations you can say to show yourself love when you need it most. For example, "I am enough."

1

2

3

4

5

FIND GRATITUDE

Of all the people in your life, the one you probably don't share your gratitude with the most is...yourself. Let's change that. If gratitude is about focusing on all that we have, then in this exercise, we are going to focus on all that we are. The more we practice gratitude toward ourselves, the more we are able to share of ourselves with others. **Finish all the sentences on this page.**

I'm grateful to myself for how I show up for...

I'm grateful to myself for challenging myself to...

I'm grateful to myself for a decision I made that...

I'm grateful to myself for taking rest when...

I'm grateful to myself for learning...

I'm grateful to myself for being quiet when...

I'm grateful to myself for traveling to...

I'm grateful to myself for speaking out when...

CONTINUED →

I'm grateful to myself for taking up...

I'm grateful to myself for reaching out to...

I'm grateful to myself for letting go of...

I'm grateful to myself for loving...

I'm grateful to myself for dreaming of...

I'm grateful to myself for walking away from...

I'm grateful to myself for never settling on...

I'm grateful to myself because...

I'm grateful to myself for accepting...

I'm grateful to myself because...

I'm grateful to myself for becoming stronger in...

I'm grateful to myself because...

CONSIDER WHAT YOU ARE WORTHY OF

Some people have been brought up to believe they need to earn love from others—that love comes with conditions. But that's not true. It's time to consider the love you are worthy of. Complete the following prompts:

The love I am worthy of looks like...

_____
_____
_____
_____
_____
_____

The love I am worthy of feels like...

_____
_____
_____
_____
_____
_____

The love I am worthy of does not depend on...

_____
_____
_____
_____
_____
_____

AHA MOMENTS...

You've been paying attention to yourself, noticing what goes on inside you, what grounds you, what excites you. This self-knowledge is your map to self-acceptance and self-love. **Take a moment to reflect on what you discovered about...**

The parts of yourself that you respect and are grateful for that you could remind yourself of on a tough day:

_____

_____

_____

_____

_____

_____

_____

_____

_____

_____

The places in yourself where you feel incomplete:

_____

_____

_____

_____

_____

_____

_____

_____

_____

_____

The ways in which you might make yourself whole:

_____

_____

_____

_____

_____

_____

_____

_____

_____

_____

_____

_____

_____

_____

_____

_____

_____

_____

_____

_____

_____

_____

If you prioritize yourself,
you are going to save yourself.

—GABRIELLE UNION

SOMETHING TO THINK ABOUT:

Because tomorrow is never promised, these exercises point us toward accepting and then celebrating ourselves just where we are *right now*.

Notes

Notes

_____

_____

_____

_____

_____

_____

_____

_____

_____

_____

_____

_____

_____

_____

_____

_____

_____

_____

_____

_____

_____

_____

_____

_____

_____

_____

_____

_____

> **66**
>
> **Surround yourself with people who are only going to lift you higher.**
>
> —OPRAH

CHAPTER THREE
Seeing Others Clearly

I've said it before and I'll say it again now: One of the most important lessons Maya Angelou ever taught me was "When people show you who they are, believe them." When the person who made you a promise fails to show up without an explanation or apology, when you are mistreated, when someone shows you a lack of integrity or dishonesty, know that this will be followed many, *many* other times that will come back to haunt or hurt you. So believe them the first time—and if you can't do that (and it's hard, I know), at least don't wait for the 29th time. In the same way, when someone shows up with intention and grace, trust and loyalty, believe *them*. Because those are the people who provide the space for you to expand your sense of love.

START WITH A LIST

List the people you spend the most time or energy on—romantic partner, family members, friends, your "work spouse," or neighbors.

GIVE A SECOND LOOK

Reviewing the list in the previous exercise, circle those who have done something hurtful, broken their word, embarrassed you, or otherwise let you down more than once.

The person: _____

Describe their relationship to you:

_____

_____

_____

Describe a time this person did something hurtful:

_____

_____

_____

How did you respond?

_____

_____

_____

What did you hope would happen? Did they change their behavior in the way you wished?

_____

_____

_____

_____

_____

CONTINUED →

The person: _____

Describe their relationship to you:

_____

_____

_____

_____

Describe a time this person did something hurtful:

_____

_____

_____

_____

How did you respond?

_____

_____

_____

_____

What did you hope would happen? Did they change their behavior in the way you wished?

_____

_____

_____

_____

_____

_____

The person: _____

Describe their relationship to you:

_____

_____

_____

_____

Describe a time this person did something hurtful:

_____

_____

_____

_____

How did you respond?

_____

_____

_____

_____

What did you hope would happen? Did they change their behavior in the way you wished?

_____

_____

_____

_____

_____

_____

CHECK FOR PATTERNS

What repetitions do you see in the situations in the chart? For instance, did you make the same excuse for their behavior? (They were just tired. I wasn't clear enough, etc.) Or do you notice that several of the people share a quality (selfishness) or are in the same group (family members)?

FIND THE HIDDEN FEAR

What are you afraid you might lose if you were to acknowledge how you really feel about these people's actions? For instance, is it a sense of being needed? Or someone to spend the weekend with so you're not alone?

PERSON'S NAME	LOSS

GIVE YOURSELF A REMINDER

How might you catch yourself when you feel the impulse to explain away someone's actions? What cues can you write for each person to remind yourself to believe what they're telling you? Perhaps you can script a reminder not to say "It's okay" when your friend shows up 30 minutes late again to dinner. (Don't worry about setting a boundary with them now; we'll explore that in chapter 6.)

PERSON'S NAME	CUE

Now review your initial list of the people you spend the most time with from **START WITH A LIST** (page 50). Star those who have demonstrated trustworthiness, caring, support, and respect more than once, and complete the following prompts.

The person: _____

Describe their relationship to you:

_____
_____
_____
_____
_____

Describe a time this person did something with love:

_____
_____
_____
_____
_____

How did you respond?

_____
_____
_____
_____
_____

CONTINUED →

The person: _____

Describe their relationship to you:

_____

_____

_____

_____

_____

_____

Describe a time this person did something with love:

_____

_____

_____

_____

_____

_____

How did you respond?

_____

_____

_____

_____

_____

_____

_____

The person: _____

Describe their relationship to you:

_____

_____

_____

_____

_____

_____

Describe a time this person did something with love:

_____

_____

_____

_____

_____

_____

How did you respond?

_____

_____

_____

_____

_____

_____

_____

RECOGNIZE THE GOOD

What patterns do you see in the situations in **GIVE YOURSELF A REMINDER** (page 57)? For instance, are these people you're comfortable asking to give you what you need? Or do you notice that several of the people share a quality (generosity) or are in the same group (friends)?

_____

_____

_____

_____

_____

_____

_____

_____

_____

_____

_____

_____

_____

_____

_____

_____

_____

_____

_____

_____

_____

_____

_____

_____

_____

_____

_____

_____

_____

CAST A WIDER NET

Look again at the list of things you feel you might lose if you shift your relationship with certain people from **FIND THE HIDDEN FEAR** (page 55). How might you find someone with that quality elsewhere in your life, maybe by joining a group lesson, finding a therapist, or other examples? (In some cases, might it be within yourself?)

WHAT YOU'D LOSE	WAYS TO FIND SIMILAR CONNECTION ELSEWHERE

LOOK INSIDE YOURSELF

Martha Beck once introduced me to a concept a fellow coach taught her called "you spot it, you got it." Let's take a moment to see if people are letting you down—in the exact ways you fail others. As you review the moments someone repeatedly did something hurtful from **GIVE A SECOND LOOK** (page 51), reflect on them: Are those areas where you repeatedly let others down? What might changing your behavior look like?

> "
> You should not
> have crazy friends...
> but sane and
> uplifting friends.
>
> —ANNE SEXTON

AHA MOMENTS...

As you take another look at the exercises in this section, **what were your aha moments around...**

The people you choose to surround yourself with?

_____
_____
_____
_____
_____
_____
_____
_____
_____

Your role in choosing them?

_____
_____
_____
_____
_____
_____
_____
_____
_____

The ways you might see them more clearly?

_____

_____

_____

_____

_____

_____

_____

_____

_____

_____

_____

_____

_____

_____

_____

_____

_____

_____

_____

> ## No person is your friend who demands your silence or denies your right to grow.
>
> **–ALICE WALKER**

Notes

Notes

" We all want to feel we matter to somebody.

–OPRAH

CHAPTER FOUR

Giving Your Attention

Making time for someone—and giving them your full, uninterrupted attention—is not easy these days. But it is a gift. This, I know for sure. When you connect with the people you most care about, you're offering them a prized possession: your attention. Whether it's in person, on a video call, in a handwritten note, or through a text message—your focus on them, and no one else, powerfully demonstrates your love for them. On the other hand, small things—"just a quick text" in the middle of a lunch or a glance at your email during a phone call with your partner (can't we all tell when someone's distracted?)—says clearly that you find any and everything else more important than the person you're with. So in these busy days, when it's so easy to multitask and even easier to allow hours or weeks to slip by, let's take the first step toward carving out opportunities to give your complete attention to those you love.

BREAK DOWN THE WEEK

"Busy" is both the truth and the excuse of why we don't spend more time with the people we love. Let's look at where your time is focused and see if you'd like to shift some hours to connect more often and more intentionally with the people in your life.

List the primary activities of your week. (We've added suggestions to get you started. If they aren't right, just cross them out.)

HOURS SPENT PER WEEK	ACTIVITY
	Getting/eating food
	Working
	Sleeping
	Talking with friends
	Entertainment (reading/videos/games)
	Childcare/eldercare
	Spiritual practice
	Exercise
	Commuting

TOTAL:
168 HOURS

> **Attention is the most basic form of love; through it we bless and are blessed.**
>
> —JOHN TARRANT

SUM IT UP

Categorize your activities from the previous exercise using the chart below and add up the hours for each category.

MORE CONNECTED

LESS CONNECTED

Solitary activities that are good for my soul:

	hrs
_____	hrs
_____	hrs
_____	hrs
_____	hrs
_____	hrs
_____	hrs

TOTAL HOURS =

Necessary activities to run my life:

	hrs
_____	hrs
_____	hrs
_____	hrs
_____	hrs
_____	hrs
_____	hrs

TOTAL HOURS =

Activities that bring meaningful interactions with people I care about:

	hrs
_____	hrs
_____	hrs
_____	hrs
_____	hrs
_____	hrs
_____	hrs

TOTAL HOURS =

Activities with little or no connection to others or myself:

	hrs
_____	hrs
_____	hrs
_____	hrs
_____	hrs
_____	hrs
_____	hrs

TOTAL HOURS =

TOTAL HOURS

TOTAL HOURS

What's your first reaction to seeing the total hours in the MORE CONNECTED column versus the LESS CONNECTED column?

_____

_____

_____

_____

_____

To determine which activities (and the amount of time you spend on them) you'd like to shift into a different category, circle an answer for each category below. (Don't worry about how for now. We'll get to that.)

Solitary activities that are good for my soul	**MORE**	**LESS**	**SAME**
Activities that bring meaningful interactions	**MORE**	**LESS**	**SAME**
Necessary activities	**MORE**	**LESS**	**SAME**
Activities with little or no connection	**MORE**	**LESS**	**SAME**

What will change if you schedule your time more intentionally? What do you hope will happen?

_____

_____

_____

_____

_____

_____

START WITH LESS

Looking at the activities you listed in **SUM IT UP** (page 72), write down ten things from the Less Connected column that hold little or no reward for you. **For each activity, ask yourself the questions below:**

ACTIVITY	Is it important to me? If not, can I stop doing it?	Does it make my life run more smoothly? Could someone else do it?
1		
2		
3		
4		
5		
6		
7		
8		
9		
10		

Would I miss it? Or was I brought up to believe it's necessary?	If I stopped doing it, would someone be hurt? Is there a quicker way to do it?

Based on your answers, what will you be able to spend less time doing or cross off your list completely?

_____

_____

_____

_____

_____

_____

_____

_____

_____

_____

_____

_____

_____

How much time will you reclaim each week?

_____

_____

_____

_____

FIND NEW HOURS

Now use this week to experiment with time-savers that could open up your schedule for moments of connection. Here are a few to get you started, but feel free to add more.

Can you bundle life maintenance tasks?
Think about where you spend time waiting. If you're going to the dermatologist, can you take something to do in the waiting room? Could you pay bills while on hold with a credit card company?

_____
_____
_____
_____
_____
_____
_____
_____
_____
_____
_____
_____

Time freed per week:
_____

Could you adopt Gretchen Rubin's "one-minute rule" (anything that can be done in one minute has to be done right away)?
The time saved from adding the task to a to-do list or re-reading an email can add up quickly.

_____
_____
_____
_____
_____
_____
_____
_____
_____
_____
_____
_____

Time freed per week:
_____

Can you better manage your energy?
You know that time of day when you're most productive? Shut off all distractions for those 90 minutes and power through your list. Focus on tasks that would take twice as long when you're less fresh.

_____
_____
_____
_____
_____
_____
_____
_____
_____
_____
_____
_____

Time freed per week:
_____

Maybe you have other ideas to discover blocks of time previously dedicated to routine tasks or doom-scrolling. How can these be transformed into opportunities for connection?

_____

_____

_____

_____

_____

_____

_____

_____

_____

_____

_____

_____

_____

_____

_____

_____

_____

_____

_____

_____

_____

_____

_____

FOCUS ON MORE

Now, you'll make two separate lists. Start by reviewing **YOUR HEART SPACE** (page 8) and add anyone you've shared small moments of love with (the old friend you adore but only hear from once a year; neighbors you keep meaning to reach out to, etc.) and who you'd like to spend more time with.

WHO DO YOU LIKE TO CONNECT WITH?	HOW DO YOU CONNECT WITH THEM? (Examples: text, walk and talk, sending a card, offering help, going out to dinner, attending yoga class…)

WHO DO YOU LIKE TO CONNECT WITH?	HOW DO YOU CONNECT WITH THEM?

Take a moment to review the list. Everyone has different communication preferences—a friend might prefer to text, while your mom prefers the phone. Sometimes it changes based on location (if they're at work, they can only text) or phase of life (you get what you get from someone with small kids at home). But when you think about the ways you connect with these people, are you using the best method for each of you? That's the method that provides the deepest connection in the most accessible way. If not, can you cross off and replace with something that might be better?

AHA MOMENTS...

You've taken another step toward growing the love in your life—
this time, by adapting new time- and energy-management strategies.
Take a moment to reflect on what you discovered about:

The ways in which you haven't been fully present with the people in your life...

_____

_____

_____

_____

_____

_____

_____

_____

_____

The parts of your life where you anticipate obstacles to maintaining these moments of connection...

_____

_____

_____

_____

_____

_____

_____

_____

_____

The ways in which your life will grow by freeing up this time...

_____

_____

_____

_____

_____

_____

_____

_____

_____

_____

_____

_____

_____

_____

_____

_____

_____

_____

> ## The most important ability a human being can have is to direct his or her full attention to the present moment.
>
> **—ECKHART TOLLE**

Notes

Notes

Only when love is a verb and put into action does it thrive.

–OPRAH

CHAPTER FIVE
Choosing Appreciation

What helps us to love people more deeply and make people feel more deeply loved? Appreciation—keenly felt and honestly delivered. When you're able to express your heartfelt appreciation to someone, whether they're a friend, a family member, a mentor, or someone else, you're telling that person that you see them, you know them, and you value them. When we make appreciation part of our daily practice, it becomes a great enabler of love within our relationships. It focuses our attention on the delight we take in one another, the relief we find in being truly known, the hope we sorely need—all the reasons we are thankful that we walk through the world with them now.

While appreciation reminds us of the specific reasons we love the people in our life, its effect ripples out into the world: The more grateful we become for the relationships we have, the more reasons we find to be grateful in general. In our last chapter, we found more opportunities to devote to our relationships. Now we'll begin to think about how we might use those newly found moments to show our appreciation for those we care for.

TRACK YOUR APPRECIATION

When we make a habit of seeking out the reasons we appreciate our friends and family, we experience a cumulative effect. Our love shows up bigger and stronger. Take a look at the list of people you wanted to connect with in **FOCUS ON MORE** (page 78), and let's drill down to discover the reasons you so appreciate them.

(person's name) _____ **always makes me laugh because...**

_____

_____

_____

_____

_____

_____ **inspires me because...**

_____

_____

_____

_____

_____

_____ **is someone who helps me because...**

_____

_____

_____

_____

_____

_____ **always makes me feel understood because...**

_____

_____

_____

_____

_____ **is someone I can count on because...**

_____

_____

_____

_____

_____

_____ **is someone who brings me joy because...**

_____

_____

_____

_____

_____

_____ **is someone who makes me feel safe to be me because...**

_____

_____

_____

_____

_____

CONTINUED →

_____ **is someone who knows how to handle the tough times because...**

_____

_____

_____

_____

_____

_____ **is someone who makes me a better person because...**

_____

_____

_____

_____

_____

_____ **is someone who looks out for me because...**

_____

_____

_____

_____

_____

If you need more space, continue your list here.

_____

_____

_____

_____

_____

This is the time to speak the word of appreciation.

—GRENVILLE KLEISER

REMEMBER KINDNESSES SHOWN

Now let's look out into the world for examples of kindness and appreciation that you've experienced, witnessed, or heard about. Instead of trying to list them all at once, be on the lookout for kindness and record any exceptional moments here over the next few weeks.

INSPIRING KINDNESS	WHAT I LOVE MOST ABOUT IT

INSPIRING KINDNESS	WHAT I LOVE MOST ABOUT IT

SUPERSIZE YOUR KINDNESS

Look over the above list. Which words or actions inspire you? Review the list of people in **FOCUS ON MORE** (page 78) who you want to be more closely connected to. Now come up with a way to "supersize" a kindness for the following people. (Note: This doesn't involve extravagant gestures or lots of time and money— it's just a little twist, an extra thoughtfulness.) For instance, instead of sending a quick text saying you miss someone, could you share a reason you miss them? Instead of meeting someone for dinner and a movie, could you join them in an activity they love?

Name a close friend:	What kindness could you do for them?	How might you "supersize" it?
_____ _____		

Name another good friend:	What kindness could you do for them?	How might you "supersize" it?
_____ _____		

Name a trusted colleague:	What kindness could you do for them?	How might you "supersize" it?
_____ _____		

Name a beloved neighbor:	What kindness could you do for them?	How might you "supersize" it?
_____ _____		
Name your partner:	What kindness could you do for them?	How might you "supersize" it?
_____ _____		
Name someone you'd like to be closer to:	What kindness could you do for them?	How might you "supersize" it?
_____ _____		
Name someone you'd like to meet:	What kindness could you do for them?	How might you "supersize" it?
_____ _____		
Name yourself:	What kindness could you do for yourself?	How might you "supersize" it?
_____ _____		

AHA MOMENTS...

These exercises helped you hone your awareness of why you love the people you do. When we are open and alert to what we most cherish in others, our love grows larger. As you review the exercises in this section, **consider the following:**

What were the responses to the kindnesses you showed?

_____

_____

_____

_____

_____

_____

_____

_____

_____

_____

Are you finding it easy or difficult to grow the number of interactions you have based on love?

_____

_____

_____

_____

_____

_____

_____

_____

_____

_____

As you become aware (and appreciative) of the care and kindnesses shown to you, how will you pay it forward, joining the greater circle of kindness among your community and even strangers?

66

Trade your expectation for appreciation and the world changes instantly.

–TONY ROBBINS

Notes

Notes

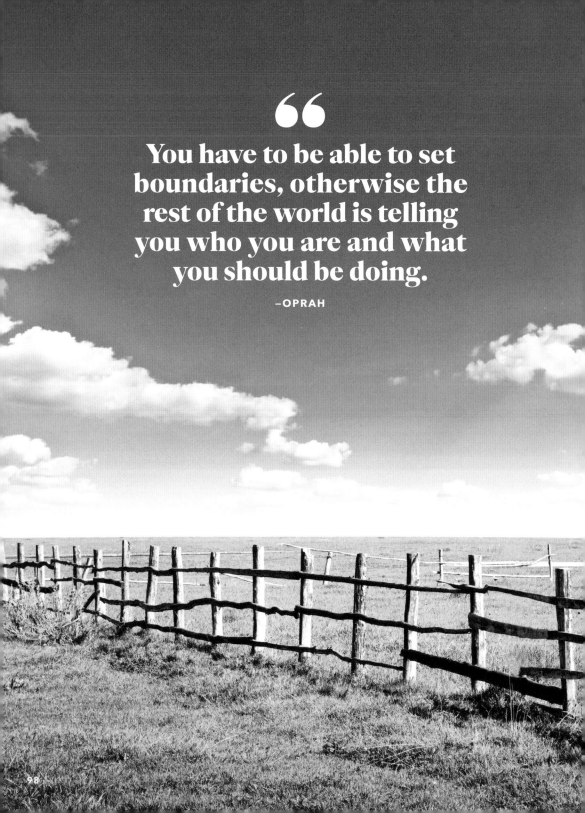

> ## You have to be able to set boundaries, otherwise the rest of the world is telling you who you are and what you should be doing.
>
> —OPRAH

CHAPTER SIX
Setting Boundaries

I have learned so much about setting boundaries over the years. For instance, author Cheryl Richardson once told me, "If you are not setting boundaries, then you are really inviting people to ignore your needs." Isn't that so true? Many people stretch themselves thin, taking care of everybody else's needs over their own. I believe setting boundaries is crucial—it's a way to honor yourself and preserve your energy for the things that matter to you. I was 42 before I figured this out—my intention had been to please others, be the nice person in the room, to say yes-yes-yes to everything. What I learned is that you can say no, full stop. Learning that was so liberating. If you're around people who take advantage or who are downright toxic—the ones you started to identify in earlier chapters—as difficult as it is, you have to find the places where you can draw a line. Does that seem selfish? I don't see it that way—you're no good to anyone else if you're not able to take care of yourself. When you're no longer living by other people's wants and needs and moods, you are able to take charge of your own happiness and your own well-being. You find that you have more love—not less—to share.

DEFINE KEY ROLES

Before we examine where a boundary might need to be set, let's write definitions for the following roles. Without thinking of specific people who hold those roles in your life, describe the best possible version of each.

I believe a good parent is someone who:

_____

_____

_____

_____

_____

I believe a close friend is someone who:

_____

_____

_____

_____

_____

_____

I believe a dedicated family member is someone who:

_____

_____

_____

_____

_____

_____

I believe a steadfast neighbor is someone who:

_____
_____
_____
_____
_____
_____
_____
_____

I believe a trusted colleague is someone who:

_____
_____
_____
_____
_____
_____
_____
_____

I believe a true partner is someone who:

_____
_____
_____
_____
_____
_____
_____
_____

CONTINUED →

Sometimes, because we want to believe the best about the people in our lives or because we aren't aware of our own expectations for them, we do not have as much clarity as we might want about that relationship. By comparing your list of people you want to connect with in FOCUS ON MORE (page 78) against the definitions you've just written on the last two pages, place names in the appropriate column:

These people meet my definition:

1

2

3

4

5

6

7

8

9

10

These people do not:

1

2

3

4

5

6

7

8

9

10

CHECK YOURSELF

While we're here, ask yourself: Do I meet my own definitions of...

	YES	NO
A good parent	⚪	⚪
A close friend	⚪	⚪
A trusted colleague	⚪	⚪
A dedicated family member	⚪	⚪
A steadfast neighbor	⚪	⚪
A true romantic partner	⚪	⚪

In which areas do I need to change my behavior to live up to my intention?

_____

_____

_____

_____

_____

_____

What is the first step I can take to align with my definitions of the role(s)?

_____

_____

_____

_____

_____

_____

_____

_____

FOCUS ON VALUES

Identifying our values can help us learn where we need to set better boundaries. After all, we teach people how to treat us. Based on the work you did in **LOOK INSIDE** (page 28), can you write down your top values and describe why each is important to you? For instance, if a value you hold is "To be a giving person," you might write that the reason is to demonstrate gratitude for what you have and to stay in a place of generosity.

	VALUE	WHY THIS IS IMPORTANT TO ME	HOW I CAN LIVE THIS VALUE
1			
2			
3			
4			
5			

NOTICE LACK OF ALIGNMENT

Look again at the list of people in your life. Who are the people who do not share your definition of each value? We often try to dismiss or ignore disappointments or conflicts with others, but these areas of discrepancy can help you to identify places where you might consider setting a boundary.

	VALUE	THOSE WHO DO NOT SHARE THIS VALUE
1		
2		
3		
4		
5		

FIND THE LINE

Setting boundaries does not necessarily mean cutting someone out of your life completely. You can love someone who doesn't meet your ideal definition of a loyal family member, but does share your sense of generosity. The exercise below is meant to help you determine where a line might need to be drawn. For instance, if someone doesn't appreciate your time and is always late, you might choose to establish a boundary in which you will not wait longer than 15 minutes for them.

PERSON'S NAME	VALUE THAT'S IMPORTANT TO ME	BOUNDARY THAT NEEDS TO BE DRAWN

PERSON'S NAME	VALUE THAT'S IMPORTANT TO ME	BOUNDARY THAT NEEDS TO BE DRAWN

AHA MOMENTS...

Before you consider how you might communicate these new boundaries (we'll cover that in chapter 8), take time to review these exercises and **reflect on any light-bulb moments you had around these questions.**

How many people in your life do you need to set boundaries with—a few? A lot?

_____

_____

_____

_____

_____

_____

_____

_____

_____

_____

What feelings do you have about establishing these new parameters within your relationships?

_____

_____

_____

_____

_____

_____

_____

_____

_____

_____

_____

_____

In which relationships do you feel your boundaries are healthy?

_____

_____

_____

_____

_____

_____

_____

_____

_____

_____

_____

_____

_____

_____

_____

_____

_____

_____

_____

_____

_____

❝

I have standards I don't plan on lowering for anybody, including myself.

–ZENDAYA

**SOMETHING
TO THINK ABOUT:**

As difficult as it can be,
setting boundaries
offers us another chance
take charge of our
own happiness and our
own well-being.

Notes

Notes

"

You get in life what you have the courage to ask for.

—OPRAH

CHAPTER SEVEN

Finding Courage

During difficult times I often turn to a gospel song called "Stand." "What do you do when you've done all you can / And it seems like it's never enough?" singer-songwriter Donnie McClurkin begins. "What do you give when you've given your all / And it seems like you can't make it through?" the lyrics ask. The answer lies in the simple refrain: "You just stand." That's where courage comes from: our ability to stand up and walk through the challenges.

At this point in your journey, you've identified places where you want to make changes to love better—more fully, more safely, more joyously. To do that, though, you're likely going to have to stand up for yourself and what you value. You might have to say goodbye to some, draw boundaries with others, or put yourself out there to meet new people to love. All of that takes courage.

CULTIVATE RESOLVE

Strength involves fitness of mind and spirit. How can we find determination, overcome setbacks, and stay centered and loving in the midst of daily life? Let's start by answering the following:

Can you create your own inner-strength team? List four or five people whose support you can enlist. How can they help you with your specific goals (for example, increased self-esteem, help setting boundaries, finding more fulfillment in your relationships). Include what you need from each person (an occasional sounding board, daily call or text, paid advice or coaching).

NAME	REASON FOR ASKING THEIR SUPPORT	WHAT YOU NEED FROM THEM

LEAN IN TO VULNERABILITY

We started this chapter with an exercise that identifies places where you could ask for help. This approach to finding courage draws on the work of Brené Brown, who says that "courage is born out of vulnerability."

Look back over the past few chapters to identify opportunities where you failed to share the appreciation you felt for someone or you weren't able to set a boundary. Can you list five areas in which you felt vulnerable and describe the feelings/physical sensations of each instance?

I was vulnerable when...   **It felt like...**

_____   _____

_____   _____

I was vulnerable when...   **It felt like...**

_____   _____

_____   _____

I was vulnerable when...   **It felt like...**

_____   _____

_____   _____

I was vulnerable when...   **It felt like...**

_____   _____

_____   _____

I was vulnerable when...   **It felt like...**

_____   _____

_____   _____

DISCOVER THE SOURCE OF HESITATION

You know that moment when you're about to smile, say something kind, or ask a question—but you don't? That impulse to withhold your best self is getting in the way of your love. Let's discover the reasons you hold back—and help you to find the courage to step forward.

**Check the explanations below that sound true for you on occasion.
Add any others we didn't think of.**

- ○ I was jealous.
- ○ I was afraid I'd be laughed at.
- ○ I didn't want to make a mistake.
- ○ I didn't think it mattered.
- ○ I felt uncomfortable.
- ○ I wasn't important enough.
- ○ I was angry.
- ○ They wouldn't appreciate it.
- ○ _____
- ○ _____
- ○ _____
- ○ _____

What you risk reveals what you value.

—JEANETTE WINTERSON

For every excuse you checked, can you list a time when you found the courage to say what you felt? What happened, and how did you feel?

_____

_____

_____

_____

_____

_____

_____

_____

_____

_____

_____

_____

_____

If you don't have examples of finding courage, can you take a moment to explain how you might approach a similar situation in the future through the lens of vulnerability? It might help to share the reason for your hesitation. For instance, instead of sitting quietly, you might decide to give a speech at a friend's wedding by starting off saying "You two know I don't love public speaking, but I so want to congratulate you on this special day"?

_____

_____

_____

_____

_____

_____

_____

FIND YOUR SOURCE

Faith can move mountains (especially faith in oneself), so let's take a moment to explore these sources of strength by answering the following:

Do you feel connected to a source of spiritual strength? What is your faith or spiritual practice? If you have none, what do you do when in need of hope? Think about how you connect with spiritual feelings, what attracts you to your faith, and what you value about your faith or spiritual practice.

_____

_____

_____

_____

_____

_____

Are you in touch with your own inner reserves of strength? Can you list four ways in which you might boost those reserves?

1

2

3

4

In moments of conflict or fear, it helps to center ourselves. Try this breathing exercise the next time you feel stressed.

> Place one hand on your belly and one on your chest.
>
> ———
>
> Take a deep inhale through your nose for a count of four, filling your belly up like a balloon. The hand on your stomach should rise, while the one on your chest stays still.
>
> ———
>
> Take a slight pause at the top of the inhale, and then release the air from your belly for a count of four, feeling the hand on your stomach lower to its original position.
>
> ———
>
> Practice this breathing exercise for three to five minutes, taking long, deep breaths into your abdomen.

How did you feel afterward? Can you describe the effect this exercise had on how prepared you felt for the challenging conversation or difficult moment you had?

_____

_____

_____

_____

_____

_____

In a changing world, an open mind might be your strongest ally. How do you respond to novel ideas? What does it take to change your mind? Does that seem reasonable or are there changes you might make to ensure you are not closing yourself off?

_____

_____

_____

_____

_____

_____

AHA MOMENTS...

It's not true that people with courage don't ever feel doubt, fear, or exhaustion. They do, but in the toughest moments, they have faith that if they take just one step more, they'll learn some of the most profound lessons life has to offer. **What did you learn about...**

What it means to have courage?

_____

_____

_____

_____

_____

_____

_____

_____

_____

_____

What it means to overcome fear?

_____

_____

_____

_____

_____

_____

_____

_____

_____

_____

_____

What it means to stand within your own vulnerabilities?

_____

_____

_____

_____

_____

_____

_____

_____

_____

_____

_____

_____

_____

_____

_____

_____

_____

_____

_____

_____

_____

_____

Sometimes being brave means letting everyone down but yourself.

—GLENNON DOYLE

SOMETHING TO THINK ABOUT:

What can you do?
What daring, brave,
unconventional,
adventurous, aspiring,
and inspiring dream
can you behold?

Notes

Notes

"

Great communication begins with connection.

—OPRAH

CHAPTER EIGHT

Improving Communication

I believe three of the most important words anyone can say are not "I love you," but "I hear you." I've learned that the most effective method for finding common ground is to approach a person with heartfelt compassion and ask "What is it that you really want?" It's amazing what they will tell you. The flip side, of course, is making yourself heard—what *you* really want—your hopes, your dreams, your boundaries, your vulnerabilities, the things you need, the things you absolutely do *not* need. In earlier chapters, you worked on seeing the people you love more clearly— who they really are (for better or worse), what you most appreciate about them. You sought out ways to find more time, and you mapped the boundaries that have been missing in your life. The next—and maybe most important—step is to learn how to communicate with clarity. That means being clear, direct, and kind. Once you have clarity, you can both listen with your whole soul and express your full self.

MAP WHERE YOU ARE

Communicating with loved ones can be challenging. While we are all on a journey, some of us are on different paths. And even those who travel our path may not be in the same place on that journey. Before we begin reaching out to others, what reminders can you list for yourself to listen and speak from a place of love and not ego? For example, "Just because I've learned what's best for me does not mean I know what's best for someone else."

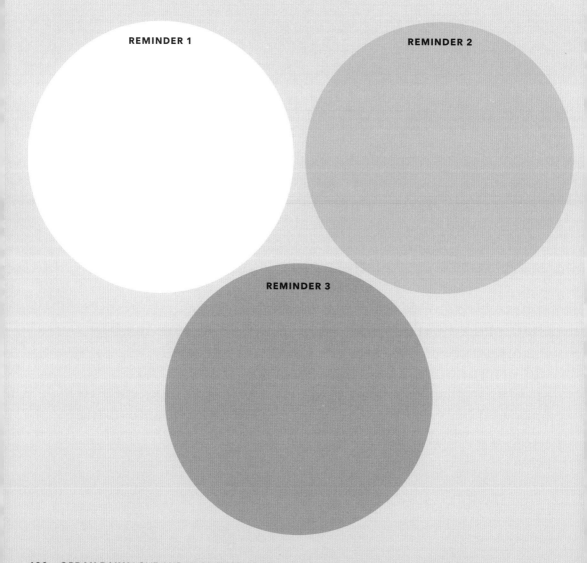

REMINDER 1

REMINDER 2

REMINDER 3

GATHER YOUR CUES

In chapter 6, we talked about how setting boundaries requires clarity—figuring out if you need to hold firm in certain situations or to cut someone out of your life completely. Now we'll work on the ways you can communicate your decisions. Shonda Rhimes once told me that she has learned to say "No, I'm not able to do that." I told her I was going to steal that line. What other words or phrases might help you have a difficult conversation around setting boundaries that are healthy and respectful, not shaming or from a place of anger?

TYPE OF CONVERSATION OR SITUATION	LINE THAT WOULD HELP ME STAND FIRM

DRAFT A PLAN

Now let's create a road map that brings together all our learnings to set healthy boundaries. List the person in column 1, the boundary you'd like to set in column 2, and the line that will help you hold your ground in column 3.

PERSON	BOUNDARY	LINE THAT WILL HELP ME

ADD A REASON

In **SUPERSIZE YOUR KINDNESS** (page 92), you made a list of people you think of but don't always connect with and determined the best way to contact them. All that's left is the actual communicating. A casual "Hey, do you want to grab a bite?" always works, but it's nearly as easy to add a "because" to your invitation that makes the recipient feel even more loved.

In the left column, write the name of the people you'd like to connect with, and in the right column, note your "because." These could include: "I could use your perspective" or "I saw this thing that always makes me think of you" or "I heard the nicest thing about you and thought you should know."

PERSON	BECAUSE
_____	I miss you _____
_____	I could use your perspective _____
_____	No one can make me laugh like you _____
_____	I have so much I want to tell you _____
_____	I heard the nicest thing about you and thought you should know
_____	_____
_____	This always makes me think of you _____
_____	_____
_____	_____
_____	_____
_____	_____

Telling the truth is not just what you say. It's how you show up.

—INDIA.ARIE

HOLD THEIR HEART

Beyond joyful conversations are the talks with the people you love who are in pain. Thích Nhất Hanh once said that compassionate deep listening lessens someone's suffering—be it sadness, anger, or despair: "The only purpose is to help them empty their heart." Think back to a recent time when someone revealed their hurt to you.

Describe what went through your head as they spoke.

_____
_____
_____
_____
_____
_____

What emotions were you feeling as they spoke?

_____
_____
_____
_____
_____
_____

How did you respond to what they said?

_____
_____
_____
_____
_____
_____
_____

CHOOSE WITH CARE

Cross out any responses that you believe might make someone sharing their struggle feel even worse.

1. "Don't let them see you like this."

2. "I know what you're feeling."

3. "Something similar happened to me."

4. "Of course you're upset."

5. "It could be worse."

6. "I hear you."

7. "This is how you can make it better."

8. "I really don't know what to say right now."

9. "I'm here for you whenever you need me."

10. "You'll feel better in the morning."

11. "What are you going to do about this?"

12. "I'm cooking dinner tonight. Can I bring you some?"

13. "Try not to take it so hard."

14. "What happened next?"

While all of the above responses are well intentioned, numbers 1 to 5, 7, 10, 11, 13, and 14 can be less than supportive, as these phrases can make someone feel less seen and more alone. Have you ever said these things? If so, write the numbers of the responses below and then describe the feelings you were hoping to convey.

_____

_____

_____

_____

Think about the purpose of compassionate listening: to offer relief. What's one simple shift you'd like to make in how you listen and respond to someone who is struggling?

_____

_____

_____

_____

FIND YOUR COMFORT ZONE

We have so many ways to communicate—words, gestures, emotions, behavior, even the clothes we wear and the meals we serve. Does your communication style bring you the response you want in some areas of your life but not others?

List the areas where you feel good about connecting with others (e.g., at work, with family, with strangers):

_____

_____

_____

_____

_____

_____

_____

_____

_____

Do you say what you mean—or do you hide behind humor or beat around the bush? How might you be more self-revealing in your conversations to have more authentic discussions?

_____

_____

_____

_____

_____

_____

_____

_____

_____

_____

When do you feel most comfortable communicating with others? Does the format matter—would you rather write a letter than mingle at a party? Text instead of call?

_____

_____

_____

_____

_____

_____

_____

_____

_____

If you feel uncomfortable in one format, how might you gain more confidence?

_____

_____

_____

_____

_____

_____

_____

_____

> 66
> # To know another, and to be known by another— that is everything.
>
> **–FLORIDA SCOTT-MAXWELL**

TAKE A MOMENT

To be our best selves when connecting with those we love, we often need to take a moment to check in with ourselves. Next time you're about to have a tough conversation, use this breathing exercise from chapter 7 before you begin.

Place one hand on your belly and one on your chest.

———

Take a deep inhale through your nose for a count of four, filling your belly up like a balloon. The hand on your stomach should rise, while the one on your chest stays still.

———

Take a slight pause at the top of the inhale, and then release the air from your belly for a count of four, feeling your hand on your stomach lower to its original position.

———

Practice this breathing exercise for three to five minutes, taking long, deep breaths into your abdomen.

What went well when you used this exercise before a tough conversation?

_____

_____

_____

_____

What did you learn or might you choose to do differently the next time you have a tough conversation?

_____

_____

_____

_____

"

Before you speak, ask yourself: Is it kind, is it necessary, is it true, does it improve on the silence?

—SHIRDI SAI BABA, INDIAN SAINT

AHA MOMENTS...

When you communicate authentically with the people you love, fear begins to fall away, and love takes its place. It's the kind of love that wells up inside and spills out, connecting you with the people in your life in a deeper, more fulfilling way. Before moving on to the next chapter, **ask yourself the following:**

What obstacles remain to your communicating with honesty and compassion?

_____

_____

_____

_____

_____

_____

_____

_____

_____

Have you built in communication breaks so that you can replenish yourself?

_____

_____

_____

_____

_____

_____

_____

_____

_____

Have you noticed any changes in your relationships after implementing these exercises?

_____

_____

_____

_____

_____

_____

_____

_____

_____

_____

_____

_____

_____

_____

_____

_____

_____

_____

_____

_____

_____

_____

66

Learn to speak by listening.

–RUMI

Notes

Notes

> "
> **A chosen family is where you are accepted, where you are seen, where you are loved.**
>
> —OPRAH

CHAPTER NINE
Recognizing Chosen Family

I heard my favorite definition of family years ago during *The Oprah Winfrey Show*: "Family is having a soft place to fall." We would all hope that would be our born kin, but sometimes it's not. We have no say in who comprises that clan. But our chosen family, now, that's the tribe you have handpicked to be by your side through the journey of life. You're connected not by DNA but by the express intention to love and support each other. Nothing is more powerful than saying, "I choose you to love." A chosen family is your soft-place-to-land spot, the safe place where you're lifted through your challenges and celebrated for your triumphs. It's where you are accepted, where you are seen, where you are loved. My biological family is pretty small. But I am thankful for my extended chosen family—the girls from my leadership academy in South Africa, my "brother" Bob Greene and his family, Gayle and her children, and our newest, little Luca. It continues to grow, as does the love that binds us.

TRACE FAMILY TIES

Families come in all shapes and sizes. Take a moment to consider yours before answering the following questions.

What does family mean to you? What would your definition of family be?

_____

_____

_____

_____

_____

_____

_____

_____

_____

_____

_____

_____

_____

_____

_____

_____

_____

What rights, obligations, joys, privileges, or burdens come to mind?

_____

_____

_____

_____

_____

_____

_____

_____

_____

_____

_____

_____

_____

_____

_____

_____

_____

On a scale of 1 (distant) to 10 (super involved), what's your level of participation in your family? Do you wish the ties were tighter or looser?

Which of your family traditions do you want to carry on?

Who in your family are you closest to? How do you nurture those bonds? Do you harbor resentments toward anyone or have unfinished business?

How might you apply what you've learned in the prior chapter on communication to address that unfinished business in a way that feels authentic and safe?

SPOTLIGHT CONNECTION

The beauty of a chosen family is that you get to shape your own support system and the energy you want surrounding you.

Thinking of your own chosen family, answer the following:

Who holds you up? _____

Who do you feel deeply connected to? _____

Who champions you? _____

Who challenges you? _____

Who do you want to show up for? _____

List the roles that you are missing within your birth family that might be filled by your chosen family. These could include brother/sister, aunt/uncle, cheerleader, guide, teacher, etc.

ROLE	CHOSEN FAMILY MEMBER	REASON

Are there roles where you don't have someone to fill in? Where might you begin to look for that kind of support?

_____
_____
_____
_____
_____
_____
_____
_____
_____
_____
_____
_____
_____

What role do you play in your chosen family?

_____
_____
_____
_____
_____
_____
_____
_____
_____
_____
_____
_____
_____

FIND WHERE YOUR AUTHENTIC SELF LIVES

Not all of us are born into an encouraging, loving environment, but having a chosen family allows us to cultivate relationships in which we can be our most complete and authentic selves.

In what three ways are you not able to be yourself with your family of origin?

1
_____
_____
_____
_____
_____
_____
_____

2
_____
_____
_____
_____
_____
_____
_____

3
_____
_____
_____
_____
_____
_____
_____

Can you describe the reasons for each of the three ways?

_____
_____
_____
_____
_____
_____
_____
_____

In what three ways are you able to share your authentic self with your chosen family?

1
_____
_____
_____
_____
_____
_____
_____

2
_____
_____
_____
_____
_____
_____
_____

3
_____
_____
_____
_____
_____
_____
_____

In one sentence, how would you describe the differences between your family of kin and your chosen family?

_____
_____
_____
_____
_____

Whenever there is lasting love, there is a family.

—SHERE HITE

RECOGNIZE YOUR CEREMONIES

One way to express the love we feel for chosen family is to maintain traditions—or start new ones. Take a moment to consider the rites and routines of your chosen family.

What rituals have you established with your chosen family? Do you do a Friendsgiving? A Friends-Yom-Kippur-ing? A Friends-Tuesday-Lunching? A Friends-Group-Texting?

_____

_____

_____

_____

_____

_____

If you were to give a toast to your chosen family, what would it be?

_____

_____

_____

_____

_____

_____

How might you bless somebody who you've chosen as your family with your intention to love this week?

_____

_____

_____

_____

_____

> **"**
> **Things hold. Lines connect in thin ways that last and last and lives become generations made out of pictures and words just kept.**
>
> **—LUCILLE CLIFTON**

AHA MOMENTS...

As you think about who is in your chosen family and how you might continue to nourish those relationships, **describe your aha moments...**

About your role within the family you were born into.

_____

_____

_____

_____

_____

_____

_____

_____

_____

About your chosen family.

_____

_____

_____

_____

_____

_____

_____

_____

_____

_____

About who's missing from your chosen family.

_____
_____
_____
_____
_____
_____
_____
_____
_____
_____
_____
_____
_____
_____
_____
_____
_____
_____
_____
_____
_____
_____

66

Life's meaning, its virtue, had something to do with the depth of the relationships we form.

–PAUL KALANITHI

Notes

Notes

> **"**
> # Even in the most mature spiritual partnership, a mate is only there to give you back to yourself.
>
> —OPRAH

CHAPTER TEN
Embracing Romantic Love

One of the most important concepts I've ever encountered—
and one that has the potential to revolutionize the
relationship you're in (or, if you're single, create a model for
the next one)—is the idea of a spiritual partnership. The
concept was first introduced to me by author Gary Zukav,
whose work has opened the door for so many of my own
revelations and has changed how I move through the world.
According to Gary, a spiritual partnership is a "partnership
between equals for the purpose of spiritual growth."
Now, "equals" doesn't mean you do the same things or have
the same number in your bank accounts. It means that
you're equal in your value systems and in your desire
to help the other person fulfill and manifest their destiny
and purpose. That's certainly how I would describe my
relationship with Stedman all these years. We each have
the desire to see the other become the best version of
themselves. Of course, when partners agree to tell the truth
to each other, buttons will be pushed. That said, after
nearly 40 years with Stedman, I can tell you that a spiritual
partnership is absolutely worth it.

SHARE YOUR INTENTION

I learned a lot about acting with intention from Gary, who says that it's key to a spiritual partnership. Reviewing prior exercises and thinking about the state of your relationship today, what are two intentions that you'd like to focus on with your partner?

My intention in my relationship is to:

My intention in my relationship is to:

Think about recent interactions with your partner: Where did your words and actions fail to align with those intentions? (For instance, do you want to support your partner's health but order calorie-loaded takeout? Did you seek more connection with your partner but phrase it as a complaint, such as, "You never spend time with me"?)

WORDS

ACTIONS

How in the future could you reframe these words and actions to better support your intentions within the relationship?

TURN YOUR ATTENTION

When I interviewed relationship expert and author Esther Perel, she said that any time you ask if you are with the right partner, you need to ask yourself, "Am I being the best partner? The type of partner someone would want to be with?" It's so easy to think love is about the other person, but as Esther says, it's also about who you are.

Start by listing the key things you'd like from your partner:

_____

_____

_____

_____

_____

_____

_____

_____

Esther also says that if you want to change the other person, you should change yourself first. For instance, if you want them to be more responsive to your needs, you might start by responding to their needs. Now review the list above and list the ways you might demonstrate the qualities you'd like.

_____

_____

_____

_____

_____

_____

_____

_____

LOOK BACKWARD

Harville Hendrix, who developed a form of couples therapy, once told me that problems that repeat in a relationship are almost always not about what's happening in the moment. This exercise will help surface how the past influences your present.

What are the top four issues that come up again and again between you and your partner?

1	2
3	4

Think back and describe the relationship you had with your parents—the feelings and energy exchange—and how that impacted you. For instance, if above you wrote that your partner complains about the silent treatment, can you find an echo in your childhood? Perhaps your parents withdrew from you instead of talking things through and you learned that's the only way to express disappointment.

66

People think a soul mate is your perfect fit, and that's what everyone wants. But a true soul mate is a mirror, the person who shows you everything that's holding you back, the person who brings you to your own attention so you can change your life.

—ELIZABETH GILBERT

REVEAL UNSHARED TRUTHS

Another part of a spiritual partnership is telling the truth—including the realizations about the conflicts you listed in the previous exercise.

What is something important that you think or feel that you have not shared with your partner?

What does your partner believe you think and feel about it?

What has your partner said or done as a result of this false belief?

How has that affected your relationship?

What prevents you from telling them the truth?

What proof do you have that your partner would react that way?

What would you like to see happen if you cleared up the misunderstanding?

AHA MOMENTS...

Through a spiritual partnership, you become more responsible, more aware, and more yourself. As you review the exercises in this chapter, **can you share how you feel about:**

Fully accepting your partner as they are within a spiritual partnership?

_____

_____

_____

_____

_____

_____

_____

_____

_____

Fully accepting your commitments to a spiritual partnership?

_____

_____

_____

_____

_____

_____

_____

_____

_____

_____

_____

Fully accepting the need for truth within a spiritual partnership?

_____

_____

_____

_____

_____

_____

_____

_____

_____

_____

_____

_____

_____

_____

_____

_____

_____

_____

_____

_____

_____

66

We do not find the meaning of life by ourselves alone—we find it with another.

–THOMAS MERTON

Notes

Notes

> "I'm in awe of good parents—those heroes all around me who sacrifice daily out of love for their children.

—OPRAH

CHAPTER ELEVEN
Redefining Parenthood

The girls at the Oprah Winfrey Leadership Academy for Girls in South Africa who came to the United States for college—I call them my daughter-girls—are a part of my chosen family. Some have parents, others don't. They have siblings, aunts, and uncles. And of course, they have each other. But they also have me. I am so grateful to be able to give them the chance to see the best of themselves and all that is possible in life with an open mind and an open heart. I always tell them that their happiness is my greatest reward. I know that's how most parents feel (I've always said parenting is the toughest job out there). But seeing the girls growing, striving, and living their best lives is truly the gift. I believe the choice to become a parent is the choice to become one of the greatest spiritual teachers there is. I know for sure there are few callings that are more honorable. If you have a parent, are a parent, or find yourself providing volunteer parenting, consider what those unique relationships can teach us about love.

SEEK CLARITY

Let's begin by answering the following questions:

**Who were your parents to you? Nurturers? Underminers? Absentees?
Confidantes? Cheerleaders? Role models?**

_____

_____

_____

_____

_____

_____

What didn't you get from your parents? How can you make it up to yourself?

_____

_____

_____

_____

_____

Who are you to your parents? What role do you play in their lives?

_____

_____

_____

_____

_____

_____

How can you bring your relationship into the present, as two adults, as equals? What would you need to let go of to make that happen?

_____

_____

_____

_____

_____

_____

_____

_____

What boundaries do you need to set? What have you learned about how you might communicate your needs with intention and without frustration?

_____

_____

_____

_____

_____

_____

If you can't change the relationship, is it possible to accept that your parents did the best that they knew how? What obstacles stand in the way of accepting that fact?

_____

_____

_____

_____

_____

_____

_____

_____

RECOGNIZE THEIR GIFTS

For the next few questions, let's consider a broader definition of parents—and parenting.

Make a list of all the "parents" in your life. What have you gained from each?

PARENT FIGURE	WHAT THEY GAVE ME

How would you describe "good parenting" and what it means to you?

CHOOSE DELIGHT

Now let's shift from the parenting that you've received to the opportunities for you to provide that kind of love and support to someone.

In what ways do you express your desire for parenting? Are you a parent or a guardian? A godparent? A mentor?

Toni Morrison said, "When a child walks in the room, your child or anybody else's child, do your eyes light up? That's what they're looking for." What is your biggest delight in the children in your life? How often do you look for what you love about them versus how often you look to improve or criticize them?

THINK ABOUT YOURS VERSUS THEIRS

I'm always mindful of something Dr. Shefali says about conscious parenting: "Love without consciousness becomes control." She helped me to an aha moment about running my school and being a mother to many of the girls in that school. Thanks to Dr. Shefali, I learned that the number one thing I could let go of is my expectations. To be clear, it's not that I don't want the girls to have expectations for themselves. It's that I'm letting go of my expectations for what will make them happy and successful.

As a parent or parent figure, what are your current expectations for the children in your life?

_____

_____

_____

_____

_____

Reviewing your answers to the previous question, are those goals yours...or theirs? In that list, place an "X" next to the goals that are yours. How can you reset your approach and help each child to find their own expectations?

_____

_____

_____

_____

_____

In the face of the deepest challenges confronting the children in your life, what can you do to offer a space where they know they are loved without imposing your dreams or trying to control their decisions?

_____

_____

_____

_____

_____

> **Parents are teachers, guides, leaders, protectors, and providers for their children.**
>
> —IYANLA VANZANT

AHA MOMENTS...

As you reflect on the parents you had and the parent (or parent figure) you are (or want to be), **review these exercises and think about...**

Was this chapter more or less difficult than others?

_____

_____

_____

_____

_____

_____

_____

_____

_____

_____

_____

Which was the most challenging question in this chapter to answer?

_____

_____

_____

_____

_____

_____

_____

_____

_____

_____

_____

_____

If you're not a parent, what notes would you want to keep in mind for any parent-like roles you might take on?

_____

_____

_____

_____

_____

_____

_____

_____

_____

_____

_____

_____

_____

_____

_____

_____

_____

_____

_____

Teach your children how to identify their own strengths. Challenge them to contribute these strengths to others.

—MARCUS BUCKINGHAM

Notes

Notes

66

In the final analysis of our lives, the only thing that will have any lasting value is whether we've loved others and whether they've loved us.

—OPRAH

CHAPTER TWELVE

Practicing Loving-kindness

Jon Kabat-Zinn says mindfulness is a gateway into the full dimensionality of being human. I love that, don't you? A mindfulness practice—dedicating time to finding quiet moments where we can be observers of our lives without judgment—gives each of us a place to connect to something deeper within ourselves. I've discovered that it's a place available to us at every moment. I remember one particular mindfulness session—years ago—when I thought about the circle of all the people who've shown me kindness: from teachers to friends to all the guests and audience members. It's a lot of people. Yet I realize that many of them, like the hundreds I met on my show every day or those who connect with us during our Oprah Daily "The Life You Want" classes, are not even people I really know. Still, I carry with me a deep feeling that I have been kept afloat by spirits of kindness. What I have found is that when you slow down your thoughts, and when you make room for the quiet moments and allow yourself to feel what actually happens, life gets exponentially better. I walk away from these quiet moments feeling fuller than when I began: full of hope, a sense of contentment, and deep joy. I know for sure that even in the daily craziness that bombards us from every direction, there is—no matter what—the constancy of stillness. It's not easy: In a poll of 20,000 Oprah Daily readers, 75 percent of the respondents said they are distracted and unable to live in the moment. But it's in stillness and time without distractions that we can find a true state of clarity—and only from that space can we find the way to authentically love those in our lives and in our world.

TAKE A BREATH

We need to slow down in order to show up, so before we begin, let's focus on a breathing exercise that might help you center yourself.

Focus your attention on your breath, the inhale and exhale.

———

Start by taking an exaggerated breath: a deep inhale through your nostrils (three seconds), hold your breath (two seconds), and a long exhale through your mouth (four seconds).

———

Simply observe each breath without trying to adjust it; it may help to focus on the rise and fall of your chest or the sensation though your nostrils. If your mind wanders, it's okay; just notice that this is happening and gently bring your attention back to your breath.

Make a few quick notes about how you're feeling right now compared to before you did the exercise.

_____

_____

_____

_____

_____

_____

_____

_____

_____

_____

REMEMBER YOUR SPIRIT

Over the years, I've spoken to the poet Mark Nepo, who says the ongoing question for us is how we can identify the conditions, practices, or experiences that allow us to see past the distractions of daily life to get to the life of the spirit. He says it's individual for each of us—listening to a specific piece of music, sitting on a favorite bench, looking into the eyes of a cherished pet. What are the ways you can find that place?

NAME OF PLACE	WHY IT CAN LEAD YOU TO A PLACE OF STILLNESS

What time of day can you carve out a few minutes to begin this practice?

_____

_____

_____

When will you begin?

_____

_____

_____

REIMAGINE YOUR HEART

Mark Nepo also says, "Our heart is the strongest muscle and resource we have." Mark recommends this exercise to help you connect more fully to your heart and the power (physical and mental) that it provides. Describe your heart in the following ways.

A part of nature (like a nest, a cliff)

A home (a glass house by the sea, a log cabin)

A musical instrument or tool (a flute, a hammer)

> **When in doubt about what to do...be loving.**
>
> —ELIZABETH LESSER

THE LOVINGKINDNESS MEDITATION

The lovingkindness practice derives from a type of Buddhist meditation that sends positive energy toward others. This five-part exercise begins with silent mantras to be said for expanding circles of people in our lives. You might want to take a photograph of this to carry on your phone to practice during the times you've carved out or when you have unexpected free moments.

Find a quiet spot and close your eyes.

Start by repeating silently,
"May I be happy. May I be safe. May I live with ease."

After a few minutes, begin silently offering the phrases to someone you respect and love, a mentor or good friend.
"May you be happy. May you be safe. May you live with ease."

Following that, choose someone you feel fairly neutral toward (your regular barista, your mail carrier):
"May you be happy. May you be safe. May you live with ease."

Now think about someone you've had a difficult interaction with—either because of your own failures or something hurtful they've done. This part of the meditation can be hard, but experts say this is the place where we deeply contact our capacity for lovingkindness. Think of this person while repeating:
"May you be happy. May you be safe. May you live with ease."

Finally, offer the next moment to everyone who shares our planet:
"May you be happy. May you be safe. May you live with ease."

What emerged from this practice of paying attention?

_____

_____

_____

_____

_____

_____

_____

What was the most difficult part of the practice?

_____

_____

_____

_____

_____

_____

_____

_____

How did it expand the love you feel within your life?

_____

_____

_____

_____

_____

_____

_____

_____

AHA MOMENTS...

Living with mindfulness allows us to experience the world in a more engaged way. When we develop the habit of noticing our intentions, we have a much better compass with which to navigate our lives. As we close out this chapter, **take a moment to note the following:**

What parts of your relationships and the world do you feel more engaged with?

_____

_____

_____

_____

_____

_____

_____

_____

Were you able to access more moments of calm with these exercises?

_____

_____

_____

_____

_____

_____

_____

_____

_____

In what ways has your capacity for love and kindness expanded?

_____

_____

_____

_____

_____

_____

_____

_____

_____

_____

_____

_____

_____

_____

_____

_____

_____

_____

_____

_____

66

The extraordinary is waiting quietly beneath the skin of all that is ordinary.

–MARK NEPO

Notes

Notes

Love Inventory: Reflection

Now that you've dedicated the time
to bringing more love into your life
and becoming more connected to loved
ones and to the wider world, take
this as an opportunity to revisit and
update your love inventory.

> **"**
>
> **I believe that every
> single event in life happens
> as an opportunity
> to choose love over fear.**
>
> **—OPRAH**

IDENTIFY THE LOVE YOU HAVE TODAY

To start, check off all the instances of love that you've experienced recently. These could be encounters with friends, family, your partner, a trusted colleague, or a stranger. For instance, when someone...

- Gave you a sense of safety
- Really listened to you
- Expanded your world with new people, ideas, or activities
- Made you laugh
- Came to your defense
- Showed that they knew you better than anyone
- Was there for you
- Handled things you're not good at
- Encouraged you to pursue your interest
- Was vulnerable with you
- Did what they said they would do
- Accepted your less-kind moments
- Showed kindness toward you
- Took your needs or wants into consideration
- Expressed what they honestly felt
- _____
- _____
- _____
- _____

REMEMBER WHAT YOU HOPED FOR

Looking back to the initial Love Inventory in chapter 1, **REVEAL WHAT'S MISSING** (page 16), list the types of love you hoped for and circle the ones that you've added to your life.

RECALL WHAT YOU SHARED

Now let's think about the moments in your life when you've shown love to others. Put a check next to ten of the expressions of love and respect listed below that you think are the most meaningful to the people you love. Then put a check next to the ten that are most natural for you. Compare this with the list in chapter 1: How many more have become natural over the course of your work?

MEANINGFUL   NATURAL

- ○ Listen without interrupting ○
- ○ Allow them their opinions ○
- ○ Courteously disagree ○
- ○ Tell them the truth ○
- ○ Apologize when you're wrong ○
- ○ Let them know if they've offended you ○
- ○ Celebrate their wins ○
- ○ Keep your word ○
- ○ Offer help when it seems appropriate ○
- ○ Give them room to learn from mistakes ○
- ○ Keep them in the loop/informed ○
- ○ Be patient/hold your temper ○
- ○ Validate their point of view and contributions ○
- ○ Keep their secrets ○
- ○ Show interest in their welfare and their lives ○
- ○ Promptly return their things in good order or replace them ○
- ○ Encourage and mentor ○
- ○ Try to understand and accept different perspectives ○
- ○ Bring an open mind to interactions ○
- ○ Be inclusive ○
- ○ Give praise freely ○
- ○ ○
- ○ ○

COMPARE THEN AND NOW

Looking at your answers above, in which areas of your life do you currently feel you are receiving/sharing love? Place a check mark in the white portion of the boxes. Now copy the check marks from **CHART YOUR ANSWERS** (page 19) and place them in the orange portion of the boxes below. Have any categories shifted to the left, toward more love? In which areas have you "moved to the left" and gained more love? Are there any areas where you would like still more love? Which lessons would you need to revisit to gain that?

	ABUNDANCE OF LOVE	ENOUGH LOVE	NEED MORE LOVE
Friends	NOW / THEN		
Family			
Children			
Acquaintances			
Romantic Partner			
Spiritual Love			

VISION BOARD:
Your Current Heart Space

Let's see how your efforts have shifted over the course of these exercises. Divide this circle to indicate where your love and attention are currently invested. Now turn back to **YOUR HEART SPACE** (page 8) and compare your progress—and identify which areas you will continue to grow toward.

Remember, we are all works in progress. If you've identified areas that still need attention, you can easily revisit the exercises in the pages of this journal.

The Love You Want

As you wind down your work in this journal, it's time to imagine your ultimate vision for the love you want in your life moving forward. Use this page to gather images and quotes that speak to the goals you have for deeper connection, more fulfilled relationships, and love overflowing. It's no less than you deserve!

**SOMETHING
TO THINK ABOUT:**

What each of these lessons
has in common is
the potential to move us
in the direction
of our highest selves.

THE EFFORTS YOU'VE made here in the name of love will deepen your connection to yourself and to the people in your life. Through your example, you will make your world—and our shared larger world—a kinder, loving, more accepting place.

Thank you. Thank you for caring and doing work that makes a difference.

As you look back at the pages of this journal, think about the questions you can now answer through the intention of love. Questions like: How will I allow love to emerge in all aspects of my life? Where will I share more moments of love? When will I develop more love with partners and friends, among chosen family or kin, and those, near and far, with whom I share community? As you know, I believe we are all born with a purpose, and I know that our purpose is not complete if it does not include a practice of love. These pages can serve as a reminder to love others and yourself as fully as you can. As Common once told me, the most important thing is to "Let love have the last word."

Oprah

FOUNDER AND EDITORIAL DIRECTOR, OPRAH DAILY: **Oprah Winfrey**
EDITOR AT LARGE, OPRAH DAILY: **Gayle King**
GENERAL MANAGER, OPRAH DAILY: **Alison Overholt**
CREATIVE DIRECTOR, OPRAH DAILY: **Adam Glassman**
CONTRIBUTING EDITOR AND WRITER: **M. D. Healey**
CONTRIBUTING WRITER: **Nancy Hawley**
DIRECTOR OF PHOTOGRAPHY: **Christina Weber**

CREATIVE DIRECTOR, HEARST PRODUCT STUDIO: **Gillian MacLeod**
MANAGER, HEARST PRODUCT STUDIO: **Missy Steinberg Bisaccia**

INTERIOR PHOTOGRAPHY: Ruven Afanador: 2, 204, 207;
Adobe Stock: Alekss: 89; anoushkatoronto: 63;
Atipat: 10; chungking: 68; Creaturart: 139;
cristovao31: 144; dachux21: 177; DubrovinskiyM: 26;
edeshko: 71; Lane Erickson: 202; Biletskiy Evgeniy: 114;
Anton Gvozdikov: 84; joesayhello: 48; katiekk2: 124;
Kavita: half jacket, 170; Konstiantyn: 153; Idelfoto: 128;
merrvas: 5; Mitch: 163; New Africa: 6, 158;
Sergey Novikov: 110; robert: 98; smallredgirl: 187;
Sunny Forest: 44; svetamart: 20; Wheat field: 182.

Library of Congress Cataloging-in-Publication Data is on file with the publisher.

ISBN 978-1-956300-02-4

Printed in China

2 4 6 8 10 9 7 5 3 1 hardcover

HEARST

Thank you

To re-order the journal and find more great products, visit SHOP.OPRAHDAILY.COM

Unlock your Oprah Insider membership offer:
OPRAHDAILY.COM/LOVE-HAPPINESS-JOURNAL

ENJOY ALL THE MEMBERS-ONLY BENEFITS OF OPRAH INSIDER, INCLUDING:

Unrestricted access to digital content, including articles from O, The Oprah Magazine archives

Exclusive newsletter including Oprah's "Weekly Intentions" videos, plus special deals and discounts

A year-long subscription to O Quarterly magazine

Members-only invitations to video livestream events with Oprah and Gayle